D0552820

Innovative, tried and tes ˑd

A review of good practic   tering

*Clive **Sellick** and Darre*

S

Social Care
Better know

First published in Great Britain in November 2003 by the Social Care Institute for Excellence (SCIE)

Social Care Institute for Excellence
1st Floor
Goldings House
2 Hay's Lane
London SE1 2HB
UK
www.scie.org.uk

British Library Cataloguing in Publication Data

A catalogue record for this book is available from the British Library

ISBN 1 904812 03 1

Clive Sellick and **Darren Howell** are based in the Centre for Research on the Child and Family, School of Social Work and Psychosocial Studies, University of East Anglia.

Produced by The Policy Press
University of Bristol
Fourth Floor, Beacon House
Queen's Road
Bristol BS8 1QU
UK
www.policypress.org.uk

Front cover: photograph supplied by kind permission of www.JohnBirdsall.co.uk
Printed and bound in Great Britain by Hobbs the Printers Ltd, Southampton.

Contents

1

Introduction

In starting out to review innovative fostering practice in the UK, we were keen to include as many practice examples as possible from the full range of agencies. We invited staff who plan, organise, and deliver fostering services across the public, independent, voluntary and private sectors in England, Northern Ireland, Scotland and Wales, to describe their innovative work. However, we did not want to deter staff by narrowly defining innovative practice simply as something new or original. We were just as interested in fostering methods that are established, tried and tested. This review identified many examples of good practice, many of which also have the added bonus of being innovative.

In order to structure the examples of innovative and established practice we used the following six major, although often overlapping, areas:

1. Recruiting and training foster carers
2. Retaining carers and creating job satisfaction by career choice
3. Creating placement choice by using partnership working and commissioning
4. Fostering children with complex and special needs
5. Providing additional services to the children and young people placed
6. Evaluating fostering services through user participation.

Fostering has attracted considerable policy attention in recent years. Major government investment, through the *Quality Protects* initiative, has helped local authorities to address the current crucial issues in fostering, for example, placement choice and stability. The introduction of *National Minimum Standards* and the related *2002 Fostering Services Regulations* have changed and clarified the way all fostering agencies operate. Statutory inspection and registration have been introduced for fostering agencies across all sectors for the first time. Research scrutiny has also increased and there is now extensive knowledge about what works in foster care.

Many services are now built on sound practice informed by research. A National Seminar, 'Stability in foster care', in January 2003, organised by the Centre for Research on the Child and Family at the University of East Anglia, and funded by the Nuffield Foundation, brought researchers together from across the country to exchange the findings of many studies related to stability in foster care, which were subsequently shared with practitioners and policy makers.

Although extensive, our search has not been exhaustive. Staff in many fostering agencies have responded to our invitations to describe examples of their established and innovative practice. Many others have not done so but we hope that this report will prompt staff and carers from all agencies to consider their work in the light of what is described here. We have reported selectively so that where an agency is named in relation to a particular initiative, this does not imply that this is their only example of good fostering practice. However, where an agency has more than one example of innovative or established practice we have at times included these.

Key messages

- Many fostering agencies are using research evidence to make recruitment effective: local recruitment schemes, for example, word of mouth and brief articles in the local press, achieve success.
- There is innovative training practice, consistent with research evidence, about what carers say that they want: managing contact, dealing with children's behaviour, and supporting children's education.
- Information and Communication Technology (ICT) is playing an increasingly important role in key areas: training, information, and user evaluation.
- Agencies are developing a wide range of retention schemes, for example, loyalty payments, 'buddying' arrangements, stress management and services for carers' own children.
- Some agencies are providing carers with career choices within or connected to fostering. The benefits include retaining carers, using their skills flexibly, and increasing their job satisfaction.
- Partnership working and commissioning enables many agencies to improve the availability of both general and specialised placements.
- There is evidence of the growing development of specialist placements for children with complex and special needs, some of which have been researched and evaluated.
- Many agencies now offer additional services to help the children placed; foster carers themselves are satisfied when the children and young people they care for receive them.
- Fostered children and young people are consulted quite often; however, their opinions are rarely communicated to senior managers or elected members to inform policy.
- Foster carers participate in the evaluation of many aspects of fostering services.
- Parents and other relatives of fostered children are given few opportunities to participate in shaping fostering services.

3

Methodology

Postal and electronic invitations to describe good practice were sent to:

- 404 agency and other members of the British Association of Adoption and Fostering (BAAF); this included all the 22 Welsh local authorities who are their members.
- 329 agency and other individual members of the Fostering Network; this included the 14 local authorities and 3 Independent Fostering Agencies (IFAs) in Wales who are their members.
- Members of the Association of Directors of Social Services, Choice Protects Review, Research in Practice, NCH, Barnardo's and Northern Ireland Health and Social Services Trusts.
- 26 targeted invitations were made to a range of fostering agencies known for their good practice from previous knowledge, for example, Best Value and other reviews and published accounts of research, inspections and assessments, including those authorities awarded Beacon Status.
- The Fostering Network recommended 11 local authorities for further scrutiny, and for the same reason we contacted 4 NCH and 4 Barnardo's fostering projects. Contact was also made with one London borough's fostering service whose details SCIE sent to us.

Scrutiny of agency documentation took place with approximately 75 fostering agencies and telephone interviews with agency staff took place with 50 of these.

The information obtained was selective, in the sense that agency staff who wanted to share their good practice volunteered it. We filtered the practice examples in two ways: first we assessed their relevance in respect of the six key areas listed above; second, we applied the research evidence about what is known to be effective.

We used our knowledge and experience of foster care to judge whether or not to include the examples in the final selection, but we did not undertake a systematic evaluation, as this was not possible in the time available.

Structure of the review

The practice examples are described in the context of findings from the major research studies, and findings from the review, in these six key areas. The research studies are described below.

4.1. Review of the main research studies

Aldgate and Bradley (1999)[1] investigated the use of short-term accommodation as a family support service to prevent long-term family breakdown. A study was made of the arrangements and provision in four local authorities, and the progress of 60 children measured, by exploring the views of social workers, carers, parents and the children themselves.

Farmer et al (2001)[2] examined the quality and outcomes of placements for 68 young people aged between 11 and 17, who were experiencing behaviour and emotional difficulties years, in 14 local authorities and two IFAs.

Padbury and Frost (2002)[3] examined how "young people in foster care are listened to and involved, ranging from day to day decisions, to wider decisions involving policy making" (p 3). In an eight-month period, fostered young people, foster carers, social workers, fostering link workers and managers from three local authorities were interviewed: 169 interviews took place. More than one third of these were with fostered children and young people between the ages of 8 and 18.

Pithouse and Parry (1997)[4] reviewed fostering services and structures across the then eight Welsh county councils. More recently Pithouse et al (2000)[5] have used national Census data on looked after children to help describe foster care arrangements in Wales. This information is being supplemented by a research team[6] commissioned by the National

Assembly for Wales to review fostering and residential services for children.

Sellick and Connolly (Sellick, 1999[7], 2002[8]; Sellick and Connolly, 2002[9]) evaluated one large IFA from the perspectives of its own and the local authority social workers. A further survey of 55 IFAs in England, Scotland and Wales explored the sector's services, costs, size, staffing, and the needs and characteristics of the children placed.

Sinclair et al (2000)[10], Wilson et al (2000)[11] and *Fisher et al (2000)[12]* used file information to conduct an extensive study on over 1,500 foster carers from seven English local authorities, about their experiences, satisfaction, and support needs. Nearly 500 placements were surveyed from the perspectives of foster carers, social workers and family placement workers, and reviewed 12 months later. 151 foster children completed questionnaires. The study also included an intensive exploration of 24 cases, and a follow-up study 30 months later examined placement careers and outcomes.

Triseliotis et al (2000)[13] conducted an extensive two-part study in 32 Scottish local authorities, and one voluntary organisation, between 1996 and 1998. It aimed to establish the characteristics, motives, social circumstances and experiences of foster carers, and to identify and assess fostering policies, structures and services. It included questionnaires from 800 active and 100 former foster carers and interviews with 40 active and 27 former foster carers, and questionnaires and interviews with social work staff from the 32 authorities.

Waterhouse (1997)[14] conducted a postal questionnaire survey for the National Foster Care Association, now Fostering Network, and the Department of Health, into the organisation and delivery of fostering services in local authorities throughout England. Data was collected from 94 local authorities. *Waterhouse and Brocklesby (1999)[15]*, in a related study, analysed 50 referrals for temporary fostering placements in five local authorities.

Recruiting foster carers

5.1. Findings from research

There are many examples of the difficulties local authorities face in recruiting and retaining enough foster carers to provide a choice of placement. Published accounts from organisations such as the ADSS (1997)[16] and Fostering Network[17] demonstrated the significant difficulties faced by local authorities. IFAs appear to recruit more easily, and Sellick and Connolly (2002)[9] found that five times as many foster carers were joining the 55 IFAs in their survey, as were leaving.

Considerable research knowledge exists about effective recruitment practice. One very clear message to emerge from this research is that success is often related to the use of local recruitment schemes, especially through word of mouth and brief articles in the local press.

Triseliotis and his colleagues found that the low profile of fostering within many Scottish local authorities adversely affected service development, including recruitment. Local authorities may be very good at saying how green they are in the ways that they recycle waste materials or improve their street lighting, but very few publicise the need for and success of local citizens as foster carers. Recruitment was largely one-off and unsystematic with no long-term direction or strategy, and the most successful recruitment methods were local. The study found that a majority of foster carers were attracted to fostering because they had spoken to existing foster carers, seen or heard a description about fostering in the local media, or both. Foster carers in this study thought that if they played more of a central role in recruitment they could more effectively address commonly held public fears and stereotypes of fostering and social work.

Sinclair and his colleagues discovered that as many as 20% of registered foster carers across the seven local authorities were not currently fostering at the time of their study. Sellick has evidence of these dormant foster carers being recruited by independent agencies.

A useful summary of the recruitment research is available in Triseliotis et al (1995, chapter 3)[18], and more recently in Sellick and Thoburn (2002)[19], who also note that to be effective, fostering agencies must respond in an efficient and business-like manner to sustain the interest of potential foster carers. Triseliotis et al (2000)[13] have added a list of suggested recruitment strategies to their book, *Delivering foster care*, which is to be found in the Appendix to this review.

5.2. Findings from this review

Recruitment and retention of carers is probably the most important factor in delivering an effective fostering service. As the demand for foster carers outstrips their supply, recruitment has become a major activity for fostering agencies from all sectors. The *Choice Protects Review* seeks to increase placement choice for the child, by looking at, among other things, what can be done to increase the numbers of available foster carers.

This SCIE review found that most agencies deploy a range of initiatives in seeking to recruit and retain their carers. Many employ a full-time worker to implement a recruitment strategy, to design marketing material, nurture relationships with the local press, deliver information packs, and follow up expressions of interest within a guaranteed time frame from the initial enquiry being made. Increasing numbers of agencies are paying existing carers a financial reward for introducing them to a new carer.

Many fostering agencies are responding in line with the research knowledge, and we have included several examples of imaginative and innovative recruitment methods. It was in this category, understandably bearing in mind the foster carer supply difficulties that many local authorities are facing, where most examples of innovative practice were offered.

5.3. Practice examples

The use of word of mouth by existing foster carers as recruiters, and local campaigns, has been supported by:

- *Southampton*, which pays foster carers £20 for introducing a potential foster carer, and a further £200 once they have been approved and a child has been placed with them.
- *Chrysalis Care*, which pays foster carers £150 for each new approved carer they have introduced to the agency.
- *Woodside*, which pays the introducing foster carer £200 once a child has been placed.
- *Kingston* places advertisements for foster carers in the jobs column of the local press.
- *Fostering People* also does this and specifies the amount paid in fees to foster carers in order to appeal to working people, who may consider fostering as an alternative job.
- *Dudley's* use of the local Training and Enterprise Council.
- *Reading's* inclusion of a publicity leaflet with every council tax bill.
- *Essex*, a Beacon Council for adoption, has applied the lessons learned from developing adoption services to its fostering services. It provides a freephone number for callers interested in fostering, and social workers try to be as informative as possible in these in-depth telephone calls. Explanation about suitability, such as health and criminal records, as well as full information about fostering, is given, in order to minimise the time taken in subsequent and time-consuming activities such as home visits. Information packs are sent out afterwards. As a result, referrals to assessing social workers are more productive.

Case examples: carer recruitment strategies

Birmingham's fostering agency has sought to deliver a presence in the heart of this busy city, by opening a recruitment centre (known as 'the shop') whose proximity to the city centre gives it access to much passing foot traffic. The shop handles personal callers and telephone enquiries from the general public about fostering. Staff members are available during normal commercial hours – thereby maintaining a presence when the city is at its busiest – including late opening on Thursdays evenings and on Saturday mornings.

This innovation, while not new (Greenwich, for example, has used a similar approach), gives high public visibility to Birmingham's fostering service and its need for more carers.

Community Foster Care, an IFA in Gloucester, has an innovative approach to the recruitment of carers. Potential fostering families are targeted from the Gloucestershire area, including socially and economically disadvantaged areas – and account for around three quarters of their existing carers. This approach brings social and economic regeneration to the area, and jobs and training for many previously socially excluded people, as well as ensuring children remain in their local environment. The agency is a registered charity and was a Social Enterprise of the Year award winner in 2002.

One agency in the voluntary sector – *Taith Newydd*, Newport NCH, obtained a grant from the European Social Fund to support a foster carer recruitment campaign. This funding and its application were particularly innovative, and the fund was awarded for the development of employment opportunities throughout Wales. Taith Newydd emphasised fostering as a possible career for users of NCH family centres in parts of Wales where there were few foster carers available to look after local children. This recruitment approach therefore brought together two messages: first, the importance of local people fostering local children and second, the potential of fostering as a career. There has been a very good response, and as a result the agency has made a further application for EU funding.

Training foster carers

6.1. Findings from research

Ongoing training for approved carers has undergone a sea change in recent years. Preparation training is now nearly universal. In Sellick and Connolly's national survey of IFAs, 100% of those studied provided training to new foster carers. Most, if not all, of the agencies across the public, independent and private sectors, provide or make available S/NVQ training opportunities for their carers. Several studies have emphasised the importance of training foster carers in three key areas[10,20,21]:

- managing contact between fostered children and members of their birth families;
- dealing with fostered children's difficult behaviour;
- supporting fostered children's education and liaising with schools.

6.2. Findings from this review

Practice developments are reassuringly consistent with research findings. The training of foster carers has become an embedded and integral part of the overall service. Many agencies have developed training so that foster carers are becoming mentors and assessors for other carers. There is evidence of innovative practice in several agencies as we illustrate below. ICT systems have also assisted developments in foster carer training. In view of the overall positive developments in foster carer training the following examples have been selected because of the innovative edge they appear to offer.

6.3. Practice examples

- An independent fostering agency, *Kindercare Fostering*, based in Kent, has sought to go beyond the standard training package by developing two additional qualifications: the Certificate in Professional Practice in Foster Care and a follow-on Diploma, both developed in partnership with the University of Surrey.

  Kindercare's analysis of their own foster carers found that around one third of them already had a higher qualification. Thus, the NVQ route seemed inappropriate for this group and all the more so when, invariably, they already had accumulated years of experience as foster carers. The Certificate of Professional Practice in Foster Care offers additions to NVQ level competence-based learning, and the Diploma offers a route for those carers who wish to enhance their training still further.

  A modular programme has been designed with its delivery tailored to the needs of carers. The course will be available via electronic media, and will include home-based learning as well as hands-on workshops and tutorial support. The qualifications will retain, and add to, the essential features of the NVQ qualification. Key subjects will be studied: for example, child development, trauma and dysfunctional development, and managing challenging situations. In the future, Kindercare is keen to develop a degree-level qualification with the University.

- Lambeth's Children Looked After Mental Health Service provide a quick response to placements at risk of breakdown, offering direct assessment and intervention to children and carers. In addition, this scheme offers training to foster and residential unit carers on the psychology of children's behavior, and advice and support to social workers.

- An independent agency, Families for Children (FfC) has also developed a range of innovative vocational and professional education and training opportunities. It publishes brochures for foster carers and social workers, listing training events throughout the year. The 2003 brochure includes sessions on contact with birth families, challenging behaviour, and the education of looked after children, which are all in line with research messages about effectiveness. This training programme prepares foster carers who are embarking on an NVQ course.

Progression to a sponsored Diploma in Social Work course is another option, and five foster carers have qualified and returned to work as social workers, having been guaranteed jobs when they qualified. A service level agreement between *FfC* and Chichester University College includes the provision of student placements and employee access to social work training.

- *Warwickshire* is one of many local authorities to offer the NVQ Award 'Caring for Children and Young People' Level 3 to carers. In order to deliver the training it has established a specialist NVQ Training Centre staffed by a team of four. Twenty places are available each year, starting in the spring or autumn. Distance learning opportunities, supported by ICT, are available and being developed further. The Authority meets all fees and expenses, including those for travel. It has also developed further opportunities for those who have obtained this qualification to become mentors and assessors.

Retaining carers by career choice

7.1. Findings from research

The research evidence linking foster carer support with their job satisfaction and retention is extensive. This should not surprise us, as most of us can recognise the value in our professional and personal lives of respect and recognition, especially when under pressure. IFAs have performed well in this area and early research contains many examples of foster carers who express satisfaction with the support they have received[22,23].

Most of the recent major research studies refer to features of the support which foster carers consider to be important: guaranteed respite; the availability of out-of-hours telephone helplines; realistic and well-managed payment systems; easy access to specialist help and advice; reliable working relationships with social workers and opportunities for close collaboration with them, including training[2,10,13,24,25].

7.2. Findings from this review

The review found evidence of local authority specialist and mainstream fostering schemes providing foster carers with key support methods in line with those recognised as effective in the research.

ICT systems have also helped developments in foster carer support, and the Tunnel Light project in Lincolnshire, which is described later, is one example.

Many local authorities have developed payment for skills schemes. These require that foster carers demonstrate relevant childcare and other skills, usually by obtaining an NVQ. Having done so they are entitled to payment at a higher level.

The following practice examples have been selected to illustrate some innovative retention methods.

7.3. Practice examples

- *FfC* has a number of retention strategies in place. Two are particularly innovative:

  It is one of the few fostering agencies to have established an opt-in pension scheme for foster carers to which the agency contributes. Second, as a reward for long service, families who have fostered for five, and ten years, receive the sum of £1,000 each time.

  Also, the importance of providing personal knowledge and support to carers is characterised by one manager, who said he expected his managerial colleagues to:

  > "know the names of every foster carer, and the supervising social worker to know the name of the family's cat, dog or tortoise."

  As a result of these and other retention strategies, the same manager said "I can count on one hand the number of families over the past 13 years that have chosen to leave because they thought they could be better looked after elsewhere."

- Well-equipped and planned centres for foster carers have been established in both the local authority and independent sectors. For example, *Our Place* is a centre for foster and adoptive families in Bristol set up in 1998. A core team, consisting of an educational psychologist, researcher, art, play, music, dance and occupational therapists, and social workers, staff the centre with sessional staff. It is a non-profit making trust which provides a wide range of organised and informal activities for all family members in "a community that understands and accepts the joys and the difficulties that arise from looking after and adopting children of all ages".

  There is a full programme of workshops, after-school and summer activities, and a range of groups for the centre's different users. *Our Place* is open throughout the week and some evenings and Saturdays. All activities are free. It aims to provide a therapeutic environment, and encourages families to meet and support one another. The multi-disciplinary staff group enables families to have access to a wide network of therapeutic, educational, social work and other professional advice and support within the centre, and in the community by connecting with health, education and social services agencies.

- *Bexley* provides foster carers with a 'buddying' scheme of fellow carers.
- *Southampton, Leeds and Bexley* provide their carers with loyalty payments and certificates.
- *Fostering Network, Northern Ireland*, has four regional advisers, themselves foster carers who provide independent information, support and advice to other foster carers on a sessional basis.
- *Stockport*, in order to assist carers as their foster family grows, has an allocated budget to provide financial help in exceptional circumstances to extend their property.

Two fostering agencies, both in the independent sector, provide complementary therapies to their carers:

- *North West Foster Care Associates* offer stress management and aromatherapy sessions; and
- *Woodside* provides a full range of alternative therapies, from art and music therapy to reflexology.

The position of the children of foster carers has been recognised not only because fostering agencies have a moral responsibility to protect their interests, but also because their welfare has a major impact on whether or not their parents carry on fostering. Several agencies have developed innovative services for these children, such as:

- the Sons and Daughters group in *Buckinghamshire*;
- *Dudley's* 'Children Who Foster' group is run by the birth children of foster carers, offering support, social and leisure activities for these 'siblings' of fostered children;
- *Fostering Network in Northern Ireland* is developing a peer-mentoring scheme for the children of foster carers.

Creating job satisfaction
by career choice

8.1. Findings from research

Less research evidence exists in relation to this area. Many practice initiatives are recent and have generally not been independently scrutinised by researchers. Aldgate and Bradley (1999)[1] found in their study of short-term fostering that many carers had developed childcare careers for themselves, which included child minding and work in family centres, as well as fostering, and that they were generally satisfied with managing their own career in this way.

8.2. Findings from this review

There are several practice examples of agencies attempting to provide career choices within or connected to fostering, as we illustrate below.

A number of agencies have reported that they are hindered by the Fostering Service Regulations[26], which do not allow carers to take on more than five hours' paid additional tasks for the same agency that employs them as carers. In response, the Department of Health has stated that the restrictions only apply to foster carers working within the fostering service that employs them as carers; they would therefore be able to pursue a management or social worker role within another fostering service, if available to them.

8.3. Practice examples

- *Bradford* provides a part-time, flexible fostering service called *Support Care*, set up in 1996. It aims to prevent family breakdown by offering families support from foster carers for planned, time-limited periods. It was developed as a response to a shortfall in provision identified by field social workers. Traditional foster placements risk the long-term full-time removal of young people from their families. Such placements can be insufficiently flexible to meet the needs of families, especially single mothers struggling alone to cope with their adolescent, where there are difficulties related to family conflict, school problems, behavioural difficulties, mental health, drugs and alcohol.

  The aim of this scheme is to meet the needs of children and their families in a flexible way, and in so doing, it also provides opportunities for foster carers to gain job satisfaction by widening their skills and expertise.

  Support Care has given a new role to foster carers who can offer befriending, advocacy and family support as well as caring. The scheme has been widely publicised through training events, led by a team comprising the scheme coordinator, foster carer and parent as well as by publications (see, for example, Howard, 2000)[27].

- *Cambridgeshire* has developed the role of 'Fostering Service Family Worker', which was set up with the aims of maintaining placement stability, preventing fostering breakdowns and assisting in planned moves for young people. The family workers, some of whom are experienced foster carers, help carers to manage challenging behaviour and support young people with their education, often through providing one-to-one work with them. This scheme, which was funded from a local public service agreement, has been generally positively evaluated by young people and foster carers as well as by social workers.

- *Kingston upon Hull* has a short break fostering scheme, which has developed the role of carers by encouraging them to be family group conference organisers and convenors, as well as advocates and 'buddies' for young people.

- *Redbridge* operates a Flexi-Carers Scheme informed by the need to encourage recruitment and retention, provide support and facilitate training, and to widen the opportunities for carers' job satisfaction. Those with spare capacity are paid by the hour to relieve other foster carers attending training sessions, and to provide respite. Two carers also staff an evening help and recruitment line for foster carers. This provides advice and support, and information about fostering. It was reviewed in the light of experience, and the operating hours have been reduced to exclude weekends, because the key period of use is from 7pm to 11pm, Mondays to Fridays.

Creating placement choice by using partnership working and commissioning

9.1. Findings from research

There are many examples of the difficulties faced in recruiting and retaining enough foster carers to provide placement choice. Only 20% of the English local authorities in Waterhouse (1997)[14] reported that they could always offer a choice of placement for children under 10 years and only 3% for children and young people over that age. In Scotland, almost 30% of children could not be placed and a further 14% were not in a placement of first choice[13].

9.2. Findings from this review

Many IFAs and local authorities are now developing specialist schemes within their own agencies, or by forging partnership arrangements and service agreements together, in order to increase the number and suitability of available placements. Children and young people placed in these schemes include those with particularly challenging and difficult needs, such as young offenders, those with learning or physical disabilities, those in sibling groups or those who require long-term foster carers.

Several initiatives have been put in place across the country by local authorities and IFAs, and in some places voluntary childcare organisations, in an attempt to replace spot purchasing of placements with service level and partnership agreements. Some are extensive, involving large numbers of agencies where costs, services and standards are agreed and monitored.

Kinship foster care and foster placements with relatives and friends has greatly increased, from 4,900 in 1997, to 6,500 in 2001, a 34% increase over the period – this is beyond the scope of this review.

9.3. Practice examples

- *Derby City, Derbyshire, Leicester City, Leicestershire, Lincolnshire, Nottingham City* and *Nottinghamshire* commissioned *Barnardo's* to assist them in recruiting foster carers in their regions. They have also worked together to construct service level agreements with a small number of IFAs involving agreed inspection and accreditation arrangements to increase placement choice, quality and value for money.
- *Southampton City Council's* Health and Social Care Directorate commissioned tenders from IFAs for 10 foster placements. They found that the previous spot purchasing arrangements were expensive, uncoordinated and lacking in any quality assurance mechanisms. *Sedgemoor* IFA was selected following an extensive process, of scrutiny of policy and procedures, and interview. This process was driven by considerations of quality, cost and partnership working. Joint staff groups manage and deliver the service and local authority staff have been seconded to the agency.
- *Chrysalis Care*, an IFA, has entered into an agreement with one London borough and is negotiating with another to recruit IFA foster carers in those authorities, which will then be available to offer local placements. This initiative was developed to avoid London children from the two local authorities being placed long distances from home.
- *Waltham Forest* and *Westminster* are among those authorities which have negotiated the pricing, and procurement, of placements outside the local authority provision.
- The *Community Placement Scheme* (CPS) is a specialist fostering project for teenagers in Belfast. It was established in 1997 as a joint initiative between South and East Belfast Health and Social Services Trust and Barnardo's. It offers an alternative to residential care for young people displaying seriously challenging or offending behaviour. It offers intensive support to its foster carers, and its social work staff set out to "try to make things work and grease the wheels". The scheme sees carers as partners in this process and treats them with respect.

Fostering children with complex and special needs

10.1. Findings from research

This category is clearly related to the one above since local authorities often report particular difficulties in placing these children and young people. Research tells us that children in mainstream fostering placements may present their carers with very troubled and troublesome behaviour and others have significant health needs. Sinclair and his colleagues found that over half the children referred for placement in the seven local authorities in their study were described by their social workers as presenting behavioural or emotional problems, and a further 10% had a disability or health problem.

There is a long tradition of local authority and voluntary organisation collaboration in respect of services for children and young people with complex and special needs. Voluntary organisations often pioneer innovative developments which local authorities commission for these children.

10.2. Findings from this review

Developments in this area are continuing, and some schemes have been researched and evaluated. The Community Alternative Placement Scheme (CAPS), set up by NCH in Scotland, has provided a practice example of their innovative work for this review which has been evaluated by Walker and colleagues. Farmer et al's study of adolescent fostering in both the specialist public and independent sectors is another example. Many local authorities have developed their own specialist schemes.

There are many examples of collaborative working arrangements between sectors across the country. The practice examples below illustrate the range of needs of fostered children and young people, which agencies are seeking to meet.

10.3. Practice examples

- *Redbridge* has a 'specialist retained carer scheme' of time-limited fostering placements for young people with complex and challenging needs. Young people aged between 11 and 16 years are placed with specialist carers rather than with mainstream foster carers, or in residential care. The specialist carers have their own dedicated supervising social worker, train alongside social workers in the borough's Adolescent Resource Centre, and receive a retainer payment of £300 per week, whether or not a young person is placed with them.
- *Norfolk* has a specialist fostering scheme, originally funded by savings from reducing out-of-county placements. This scheme places children between the ages of five and 15. Foster carers and social workers work closely alongside staff from a local residential therapeutic unit. The support package, fees and the services for children are in line with those of nearby IFAs.
- *Find Us Keep Us* is part of the Sexual Abuse Child Consultancy Services Group (SACCS), offering an integrated multi-disciplinary approach with measurable outcomes, consisting of therapeutic parenting, therapy, life story and placement services, to aid recovery from trauma. The programme continues into placement.

Case examples: services for children with complex and special needs

The *Community Alternative Placement Scheme* (*CAPS*) was set up by NCH Action for Children, Scotland, in 1997, in response to a need for community-based alternatives to secure care and accommodation. Young people placed present a full range of behavioural problems including aggression, self-harm, prostitution, drug abuse and alcohol misuse. An evaluative study of its effectiveness concluded that "a considerable number (of these young people) can be placed in foster care and some can be helped to turn their lives around in a major way" (Walker et al, 2002, p 223)[24].

The *Wessex Community Projects* Remand Fostering Scheme is also provided by the NCH, and Hampshire, Portsmouth, Southampton and the Isle of Wight commission its services. Young people who might otherwise be remanded in custody are referred for foster placements. The staff has estimated that 75% of young people in the project do not commit further offences. The project has also developed a post-custody supported accommodation scheme.

The *Genesis Fostering Project* in Newcastle is a Barnardo's scheme which provides local authorities in the North East with planned specialist foster placements for young people "who display sexually abusive, or extensive sexualised behaviour, which is causing concern and does, or may, pose a threat to others".

NCH's *Caring Together* in Lincoln provides a combined family placement and support service. Foster placements for children with complex medical demands and challenging behaviour arising from their disabilities and support services to their families are tailored to meet a range of needs.

Providing additional services to the children and young people placed

11.1. Findings from research

Examples from research studies include Farmer and her colleagues, who point to the importance of 'appropriate counselling' for the young people in the study, most of whom were in local authority placements.

When Sellick and Connolly evaluated an IFA, they stated that:

> Children were provided with regular therapy sessions, had their educational needs championed by an educational liaison officer and could meet their family and friends in a well – equipped contact centre. (Sellick and Connolly, 2002, p 108)[9]

11.2. Findings from this review

The evidence from this review is that substantial developments have taken place in this area. These have been made possible with the use of funds from both Quality Protects and Child and Adolescent Mental Health Services (CAMHS) initiatives. It is important to note that foster carers themselves report satisfaction when the children and young people they are looking after receive these services.

11.3. Practice examples

- *Outlook Fostering*, an independent agency, is promoting child psychotherapy "to promote the child's view of their world and experience; to provide information on children's emotional development, behaviour and relationships from birth to adulthood; to promote public and professional understanding of child psychotherapy and access to child psychotherapy services". More information on their approach can be found at www.childpsychotherapytrust.org.uk

- *Hampshire* has appointed a lead officer responsible for the education of children in public care, a dedicated staff group of teachers and a community therapist for looked after children.

- *Jigsaw* IFA identified the need to provide individual therapy to the children placed with their carers as well as offering support to foster carers and teachers. It employs qualified staff providing play therapy, day respite care and classroom support.

- Another IFA, *Woodside*, commissions a 'comprehensive therapeutic assessment' from an independent provider, with the agreement of the placing local authority. This is followed by therapy and educational services.

- *West Sussex* has recruited two child psychologists to provide therapy and advice to foster carers with children in permanent placement, and this has proved an invaluable support to those caring for children with very challenging behaviour and profound attachment problems. Their 2003 Accommodation Strategy sets out how they will provide additional support and therapeutic assistance to foster carers and children.

- Royal Liverpool Children's Trust, Alder Hey, in partnership with Liverpool Social Services and the National Teaching and Advisory Service, provide a CAMHS fostering innovation. The *Rosta Project* is a therapeutic fostering service "with intensive, multi-disciplinary wraparound support for young people with complex needs". Evaluation found that it has been successful in significantly increasing placement stability and has achieved real success in reintegrating young people to education and in increasing their attainment.

- *Cheshire* has an Education Support and Development Team whose aim is to improve educational achievement and opportunity. It consists of an educational psychologist and three teachers who provide direct support and advice to children and foster carers.

- *Southwark* has a 'Care Link Team' of mental health workers providing assessment and therapy, and also good links with a local psychiatric teaching hospital. It established an education project to deal with non-school attendance, which was found to be associated with placement breakdown.

Evaluating fostering services through user participation

The users of fostering services are divided into three groups: fostered children and young people, foster carers and their families, and birth parents and other relatives. The three are considered in turn in respect of their role in participating in and evaluating services.

We note that *Foster Care Associates* (an organisation of 12 associate members across England and Wales) consulted a fourth group, local authority social work staff who commission services. They asked MORI to conduct a survey of social services managers "to measure and evaluate customer experience and satisfaction with its services".

12.1. Findings from research

Padbury and Frost's (2002)[3] study of *fostered children and young people* in three local authorities found that they were encouraged to participate in decisions affecting their lives. However, their views were very rarely communicated to policy makers at either senior management or elected member level.

Foster carers are encouraged to participate in many aspects of the fostering services and they are major respondents and witnesses in many research studies.

In the area of *parental participation*, Harwin and Owen's 2003 study[21], *Making care orders work*, found that 50% of care plans where children were to be fostered long term did not specify the parents' role in decision making, and in 75% of cases say how disagreements should be resolved despite the fact that parental responsibility remained shared.

12.2. Findings from this review

There appear to be marked differences in practice between how carers, children and relatives are brought into the participation and evaluation systems of fostering agencies.

Many local authorities have promoted the participation of children and young people in service development, using the Quality Protects programme. Practice evidence shows that *fostered children and young people* are becoming increasingly influential in many agencies. Several agencies have made explicit reference to the United Nations Convention on the Rights of the Child, including the right to participate in decisions about themselves. We have found practice examples where imaginative methods have been found to bring young people's views to the attention of managers and members.

Foster carers are encouraged to participate in many aspects of the fostering services affecting both themselves and the fostered children. Indeed they are major respondents and witnesses in many research studies. Foster carers and their families as recipients of supervision, training and support are key users of fostering services. They are also involved in the services that their foster children receive. Many fostering agencies have established and developed methods of foster family participation and evaluation.

A number of initiatives have sought the opinions of foster carers through questionnaires and interviews. These exercises are often related to actual placements so allow feedback to be more specific.

Despite our investigations, we found very few examples of the *parents and other relatives of fostered children* being brought into the participation and evaluation systems. Our experience is consistent with those of other researchers.

It is very important to note that *ICT is playing a major role* in the development of user communication, participation and evaluation for young people and their foster carers.

12.3. Practice examples

12.3.1. By fostered children and young people

- *Norfolk County Council* has a *Kids in Care Together* group of looked after young people "who are trying to improve the life and name of those already in the care system". It has an innovative web site, www.kict.norfolk.gov.uk, which contains many helpful details for looked after children and young people. The group provides consultation and advice to the department, and has a direct impact on policy and practice evaluation and change. Members of the group participated in a review monitoring the implementation of a survey about the views of Norfolk looked after children. It has produced two publications, *The view from the front revisited* and *Moving on up: Young people's views on leaving care in Norfolk*.
- *Cambridgeshire* has a *Just Us Group* of looked after children, which meets monthly, and operates in three localities. They were consulted during the Best Value Review, and contribute to designing staff training and information for other looked after children.
- *Westminster* has produced a video of fostered children talking about their experience. Together with its video of foster carers talking, it is used to inform foster carers, social workers and managers and local authority members.
- In *Kingston* a website enables fostered children to contribute to their LAC review forms as well as e-mailing messages to their social workers.

12.3.2. By foster carers and their own children

- *Cambridgeshire* has a system in place for senior managers to go back to the 'shop floor' by spending periods alongside foster carers and social workers.
- *West Sussex* foster carers are asked to comment on what works after a child has been in placement for two years.
- *Leeds* conducts exit interviews "to give foster carers who have recently left an opportunity to provide feedback on their former fostering experience".
- *Westminster* has produced a video of foster carers talking, which is used for training and informing all levels of social work staff. The

authority has also undertaken a questionnaire with foster carers, seeking their views on the support, which they value.

- *North West Foster Care Associates* has also completed a 'meeting the needs of foster carers' questionnaire with their carers.

Some agencies have established formal and representative meetings between foster carers, social workers, senior managers and, occasionally, local authority members.

- *Bexley* has a Foster Executive.
- *Warwickshire* has a Foster Care Development Group.
- *Leeds* has a Foster Care Liaison Group, consisting of the Director and Assistant Director and other managers alongside foster carer representatives. The Director chairs the group and a foster carer is the Vice-Chair. A range of topics are considered, for example, issues for Asian carers and payments for skills. Group members believe that its work has "led to a greater understanding on both sides".
- Foster carers are members of the Board of Directors in some IFAs, for example, *Community Foster Care* and *East London Foster Carers*.

12.3.3. By parents and other relatives

- The *Family Rights Group* was commissioned by three London boroughs to undertake interviews with parents of looked after children as part of their Best Value reviews. Parents from a range of backgrounds were interviewed and their views and messages to service providers informed the review. Copies of the collected messages and views of all the parents interviewed are available from the Family Rights Group.
- *Cheshire* included an evaluation exercise for 'people with parental responsibility', in addition to separate exercises with looked after children and foster carers, as a part of its Foster Care Review. Parents and others were asked by means of a questionnaire to specify areas of satisfaction and dissatisfaction with the fostering service and their responses informed a review of the service.

Some agencies have incorporated parents in the training of foster carers and social workers, such as:

- *Bradford's* Support Care.
- The former *Lothian* Region Social Work Department included parents of looked after children in preparation training sessions for foster carers which was considered helpful in developing "working relationships based on understanding and listening to one another. This in turn anticipates the kinds of negotiation and advocacy skills which will assist parents and carers alike in the formal meetings which consider and review the needs of children" (Sellick and Thoburn, 1996, p 47)[28].
- *Kingston* includes the contributions of parents for the annual review of foster carers.

12.3.4. Using ICT

Case example: using ICT to facilitate user evaluation

The Tunnel Light project set up in April 2001 by Lincolnshire Social Services harnesses the Internet to strengthen contact between social services staff (FPS: Family Placements Service, Lincolnshire) and foster carers, adoptive parents, children looked after and the general public. The creation of a website, www.family-lincs.org.uk, has been the centrepiece of the project and the delivery platform through which communication has been maintained.

The project has been a cross-agency partnership – local authority with the not-for-profit sector. 'Advice Lincs' has provided consultancy on project implementation and hosts the site on their servers. They are a pan-county advice and support service.

The aims of the project were:

- the creation of appropriate e-support between families and Lincolnshire's FPS;
- the establishment of 'e-communities' between foster families and looked after children;

- to provide alternatives to traditional education and training opportunities, the development of management policies as part of the local authority's e-government agenda and to provide the general public with information regarding access to fostering and adoption services;
- to establish an alternative means of communication in what is a large rural county.

Lincolnshire wanted to make sure that young people in public care have safe access to the Internet by providing them with the necessary technology so they have the same educational and recreational opportunities other children have in their own families.

The project initially engaged with 15 'pioneer' foster families. Selection was based on 'novice' computer users and each family was issued with a laptop computer, a web-cam, a printer and software. Participative strategies have been adopted to inform project design and roll out by engaging foster carers and young people in the design, story boarding and implementation of web-based services and overall evaluation of the project.

The involvement of foster carers and young people throughout the process provided a very valuable dimension to this local authority's thinking in terms of presentation of information to the general public, the sort of resources carers require, and their training needs.

One young care leaver was provided with the opportunity to develop their ICT skills through a NVQ training scheme in conjunction with Advice Lincs. This was intended to provide a springboard for new career opportunities.

One unintended benefit of this project has been the ability for children in previous fostering placements to maintain contact with their carers. As a Tunnel Light Project member has noted:

"... one of our [Lincolnshire's] foster children spent many years with a foster family who returned to Uganda. It was such a wrench for this little girl but they can keep in touch by e-mail, it's just brilliant!"

13

Conclusion

This review has provided a picture of foster care practice in Britain in 2003. Agencies in the public, private, voluntary and independent sectors across the four countries of the UK are represented. The six chosen categories were used to structure this examination of contemporary fostering practice and enabled us to investigate how people are alerted and attracted to fostering; what methods and services support and retain them; how fostering can provide for the needs of children and young people; and what fostering agencies can do to learn from the experiences of carers, children and birth families in order to be more sensitive and successful.

The many practice examples paint a picture of a busy, complex and demanding scene. The identity of foster care varies from place to place within as well as between sectors. Service needs are both varied and distinct and change over time. Service provision across Britain continues to be very wide-ranging. There are children who gain substitute family life in foster care, others who remain a part of their own families often because they receive supplementary foster care, such as in the *Support Care* programme in Bradford, and others who benefit from a variety of options in between.

In some places thoughtful and energetic attempts have been made to evaluate or analyse practice initiatives by asking service users what they thought and by conducting internal reviews and appraisals. Most of these self-reported accounts, however, are descriptive and very few have been evaluated by objective or independent outsiders, although to their credit some have. From within the 50 or so agencies named in this review it would be possible as a future exercise to scrutinise the effectiveness of what at this level appear genuinely innovative and successful practice initiatives.

Many participants were clear about the kinds of outcomes, which they sought from their practice and a number of these were committed to the inclusion of service users to assist them in their definitions. Might, for example, those children whose foster carers have benefited from the educational innovations of *Kindercare* or *Families for Children* themselves have better educational outcomes? This is well beyond the scope of this review's fleeting glance at foster care practice, but this review confirms the need for continued outcome studies if effectiveness is to be taken seriously.

Every fostering agency included in this review, indeed every fostering agency in the country, has been or will be externally inspected in some form or another in ways that are often experienced as stressful and all-consuming. It was entirely unsurprising and understandable, therefore, that most agencies had not sought additional external evaluation. We had the privileged task of inviting staff from these agencies to tell us what they do well and consider innovative. They were not required in this exercise to do anything other than talk about what they think is positive, helpful, popular, successful and so on. In other words this was quite a different experience than most had been used to over many years. Although we are pleased with the overall response to our approach, the silence in some quarters was probably due as much to surprise as it was to busyness.

Two particularly important issues, the use of ICT and the growth of partnership and service agreements between sectors, are having a real and growing impact on the provision of fostering placements and related services. Their influence often underpinned many of the innovative and more established practice initiatives in this review. ICT systems have assisted developments in foster carer training, for example, the distance learning model in *Warwickshire*, and support as well as in participation and evaluation systems for young people and their foster carers, for example the Tunnel Light Project in *Lincolnshire*. Some agencies see the value in having effective systems in place to deliver management information and even to facilitate the process of matching the child to carer, following referral, using the characteristics of both to inform the process, as with *Kindercare*'s Referral Management System (RMS) software.

Service and partnership agreements between local authorities and IFAs and voluntary organisations appear to have made real inroads in respect of both placement availability and recruitment. These are in all shapes and sizes involving both single and multiple agency arrangements such as the one between several local authorities and IFAs in the East Midlands. Other formal agreements provide specified local authorities with specialist services by voluntary organisations such as remand foster placements by the *Wessex Community Projects*.

A third theme, the continued development of specialist fostering schemes in local authorities as well as elsewhere, also emerged in this practice review. Such schemes are providing extensive support and retention packages to more foster families and a range of direct therapeutic and educational services to more children and young people whose experiences, needs and behaviour present significant challenges to those who care for them.

The response from fostering agencies across the public, private, voluntary and independent sectors has been encouraging. Staff members from many different agencies were keen to take up our invitation to describe their established and innovative practice. Working cultures characterised by competitiveness and secrecy are being replaced by those where agencies are genuinely pleased to share their practice and to take a pride in it. It seems to us that the practice examples contained here are largely in line with policy directions and research messages about effective, sensitive and imaginative foster care practice.

References

1   Aldgate, J. and Bradley, M. (1999) *Supporting families through short term fostering.* London: The Stationery Office.

2   Farmer, E., Moyers, S. and Lipscombe, J. (2001) *The fostering task with adolescents*, Bristol: University of Bristol.

3   Padbury, P. with Frost, N. (2002) *Solving problems in foster care: Key issues for young people, foster carers and social services*, London: The Children's Society.

4   Pithouse, A. and Parry, O. (1997) 'Fostering in Wales: the All Wales Review', *Adoption and* Fostering, vol 21, no 2, pp 41-9.

5   Pithouse, A., Jones, E., Crowley, A., Butler, I. and Smail, P. (2000) *A study of the placement of looked after children in Wales, commissioned by the SSI Wales*, Cardiff: School of Social Sciences, Cardiff University.

6   Clough, R., Bullock, R., Colton, M. and Ward, A. (in preparation) *Review of the purpose, development and management of fostering services for children in Wales and review of the purpose and future shape of residential care services for children in Wales'*, Cardiff: National Assembly of Wales.

7   Sellick, C. (1999) 'Independent Fostering Agencies: providing high quality services to children and carers?', *Adoption and Fostering*, vol 23, no 4, pp 7-14.

8   Sellick, C. (2002) 'The aims and principles of independent fostering agencies: a view from the inside', *Adoption and* Fostering, vol 26, no 1, pp 56-63.

9   Sellick, C. and Connolly, J. (2002) 'Independent fostering agencies uncovered: the findings of a national study', *Child and Family Social* Work, vol 7, no 2, pp 107-20.

10   Sinclair, I., Wilson, K. and Gibbs, I. (2000) *Supporting foster placements*, University of York (www.york.ac.uk/inst/swrdu/fosterplacements).

[11] Wilson, K., Sinclair, I. and Gibbs, I. (2000) 'The trouble with foster care: the impact of stressful events on foster carers', *British Journal of Social Work*, vol 30, no 2, pp 193-209.

[12] Fisher, T., Gibbs, I., Sinclair, I. and Wilson, K. (2000) 'Sharing the care: qualities sought of social workers by foster carers', *Child and Family Social Work*, no 5, pp 225-33.

[13] Triseliotis, J., Borland, M. and Hill, M. (2000) *Delivering foster care*, London: BAAF.

[14] Waterhouse, S. (1997) *The organisation of fostering services: A study of the arrangements for delivery of fostering services in England*, London: National Foster Care Association.

[15] Waterhouse, S. and Brocklesby, E. (1999) 'Placement choices for children – giving more priority to kinship placements', in R. Grieeff (ed) *Fostering kinship: An international perspective on kinship foster care*, Aldershot: Ashgate.

[16] ADSS (Association of Directors of Social Services) (1997) *The foster care market: A national perspective*, London: ADSS.

[17] Warren, D. (1997) *Foster care in crisis: A call to professionalise the forgotten service*, London: National Foster Care Association.

[18] Triseliotis, J., Sellick, C. and Short, R. (1995) *Foster care: Theory and practice*, London: B.T. Batsford.

[19] Sellick, C. and Thoburn, J. (2002) 'Family placement services', in T. Newman, D. McNeish and H. Roberts (eds) *What works for children? Effective services for children and families*, Buckingham: Open University Press.

[20] Cleaver, H. (2000) *Fostering family contact*, London: The Stationery Office.

[21] Harwin, J. and Owen, M. (2003) *Making care orders work*, London: The Stationery Office.

[22] Bebbington, A. and Miles, J. (1990) 'The supply of foster families for children in care', *British Journal of Social Work*, vol 20, pp 283-307.

[23] Sellick, C. (1992) *Supporting short term foster* carers, Aldershot: Avebury.

[24] Walker, M., Hill, M. and Triseliotis, J. (2002) *Testing the limits of foster care: Fostering as an alternative to secure* accommodation, London: BAAF.

[25] Kirton, D., Ogilvie, K. and Beecham, J. (2003) *Remuneration and performance in foster care: Final report*, Canterbury: University of Kent at Canterbury.

[26] DoH (Department of Health) (2002) *Fostering services, national minimum standards and fostering services regulations*, London: The Stationery Office.

[27] Howard, J. (2000) 'Support care: a new role for foster carers', in A. Wheal (ed) *Working with parents: Learning from other people's experience*, Lyme Regis: Russell House Publishing Ltd.

[28] Sellick, C. and Thoburn, J. (1996) *What works in family placement?*, Ilford: Barnardo's.

Appendix:
Recruitment strategies suggested

The following is taken from Triseliotis et al (2000, pp 256-48)[13].

Each authority is asked to consider which of the following recommendations apply to its own needs and circumstances.

Specific suggestions

- Local authorities, preferably collectively, will need to get professional advice on how to organise and promote fostering need and fostering campaigns. On the basis of what carers have said, a balance has to be struck between projecting children's needs and the job of fostering.
- Authorities should identify first what their exact foster care needs are, that is, what kind of children they have requiring foster homes, their age, possible behavioural and/or emotional difficulties, learning or other disabilities, racial and/or ethnic and cultural background and the kind of foster homes that would be needed to fit with these children's needs.
- Each authority will need to study both the profile of its existing carers as well as the population and other characteristics of their area, such as age composition, housing, employment patterns, especially for women, before deciding how and who to target.
- Give carers a central role and a much higher profile than at present, in all aspects of recruitment, preparation and training. Carers, young people with experience of fostering, carers' own children and birth parents can convey greater confidence and provide valued and accurate information helping to dispel stereotypes. They can also instil confidence in many people who are uncertain about putting themselves forward.
- One lesson to emerge from the research is that target groups have to be varied to take account of the specific area where the campaign is taking place. For example, in some of the rural areas more emphasis could be placed on the self-employed, non-manual female workers and those holding skilled manual jobs (drivers, post office workers, telephone engineers, electricity workers, plumbers, etc). Besides other groups, campaigns have to target more vigorously unemployed people and people

of lower income providing also much greater reassurance about eligibility criteria not being based on income or wealth.

- Recruitment efforts should have continuity rather than being episodic. When a campaign is being planned it is necessary to ensure that the required labour resources are also in place. The way enquiries are initially responded to and followed up can determine whether an applicant continues or not. Receptionists who profess not to know what it is all about, the person responsible being unavailable, promised information not arriving, or visits cancelled, were all found to be extremely off-putting to carers.

- Authorities should raise awareness about childcare need, with the emphasis on local need, and project fostering as a service to children, including those with disabilities, while also stressing the availability of support, training and career opportunities; and that there is nothing wrong in being paid for undertaking a very skilled and demanding job.

- Keep a balance between putting across the heavy demands of the task, including the children's difficulties, while also highlighting the professional and emotional satisfactions to be derived.

- Recognise the great potential of word of mouth recruitment. This, however, relies heavily on having contented carers. Supporting and nurturing existing carers and encouraging their identification with the agency not only helps to retain them longer, but they also become good recruitment agents themselves.

- The media can make a significant contribution to recruitment through feature articles and advertisements, especially in the local press, and documentaries and advertisements on television and local radio.

- More use could be made of community hall meetings, church meetings, and those at other places of worship, for example, mosques and temples, targeting by letter or approaching people who fall into the kind of categories that more carers come from.

- Publicity ought to stress that foster carers come from all walks of life. Those over 40 and single carers, the childless and the childfree can be targeted much more vigorously than at present.

- More targeting could be directed towards those who are already working or have worked in the social care sector.

- Special efforts should be made to attract carers from different racial/ethnic backgrounds, involving also staff from similar types of background.

- Authorities should outline the career opportunities, including possibilities for pursuing further qualifications such as NVQs or SVQ and beyond. Highlight how fostering is about team work, sharing the task and working closely with other professionals, such as social workers, teachers, residential staff and staff at day centres.

Index

Other Knowledge Reviews available from SCIE

KNOWLEDGE REVIEW 1
Learning and teaching in social work education: Assessment
Beth R. Crisp, Mark R. Anderson, Joan Orme and Pam Green Lister
1 904812 00 7
November 2003

KNOWLEDGE REVIEW 2
The adoption of looked after children: A scoping review of research
Alan Rushton
1 904812 01 5
November 2003

KNOWLEDGE REVIEW 3
Types and quality of knowledge in social care
Ray Pawson, Annette Boaz, Lesley Grayson, Andrew Long and Colin Barnes
1 904812 02 3
November 2003

KNOWLEDGE REVIEW 5
Fostering success: An exploration of the research literature in foster care
Kate Wilson, Ian Sinclair, Claire Taylor, Andrew Pithouse and Clive Sellick
1 904812 04 X
November 2003